Thoughts of The Morning

31 Days of Divine Thinking

Sharon R. Peters

Love Clones Publishing
www.lcpublishing.net

Copyright © 2015 by Sharon R. Peters. All rights reserved. This book or any portion thereof may not be reproduced or used in any manner whatsoever without the express written permission of the publisher except for the use of brief quotations in a book review.

Printed in the United States of America

First Printing, 2015

ISBN: 978-0692597422

King James VersionScripture quotations marked "KJV" are taken from the Holy Bible, King James Version (Public Domain).

Publishers:
Love Clones Publishing
Dallas, TX 75205
www.lcpublishing.net

Dedication

This book is dedicated to my Mother, Janet Stringer who always told me "*Sharon go to bed now and give your mind a rest*"! She would say that because I was always thinking. Well I learned how to do just that, I laid myself down and as I rested the Holy Spirit filled my spirit with the THOUGHTS OF GOD, thus causing me to wake up with divine inspiration and divine revelation! The moral of the story, OBEY THY MOTHER, a book may come forth!

Acknowledgements

I acknowledge my Lord & Savior Jesus Christ, who I look to as the author and finisher of my faith.

I acknowledge the Holy Spirit, who speaks and articulates to me daily the oracles of God.

I acknowledge my husband Robbie C. Peters, who treats me like a queen and who is the man God gave me to love.

I acknowledge my biological children, Shaniece and Kyle and my grandchild and prototype, Shaniya, who I endeavor to leave a legacy in print for.

I acknowledge my bonus children, who I obtained through marriage and my host of spiritual children both near and far, who bless me often.

I acknowledge my loyal personal administrator, Margaret Eason who is always ready to provide administrative support to all of my endeavors!

I acknowledge my fellow lady authors, Chara Taylor, Monica Lloyd and the Book Warden herself, Candace Ford for joining me in making sure the church is not void of knowledge in print.

Lastly, I acknowledge *the greatest place on the planet,*

The Empowerment Word & Truth Church and its membership, who serve as my spiritual family who I am blessed to serve weekly!

PREFACE

Jeremiah 29:11-13 "For I know the thoughts that I think toward you, saith the Lord, thoughts of peace, and not of evil, to give you an expected end. Then shall ye call upon me, and ye shall go and pray unto me, and I will hearken unto you. And ye shall seek me, and find me, when ye shall search for me with all your heart."

For years I have awaken with divine thoughts! These early morning thoughts have served to not only shape my day but they have helped me journey through life. In addition, they have helped me overcome many of life's ills through the downloaded knowledge of God.

My morning thoughts often expose me to the wisdom of God through the revelation behind His word!

I have learned over the years when God thinks, He plans! In other words, His thoughts equate to a plan for my life. So every morning I have trained my spirit to tap into the mind of God, which His Spirit knows, and by doing so, my thoughts become His thoughts. How awesome is this! I start my day with "My Morning Thoughts" which are divine in nature. These thoughts will shape and set my day in motion!

Almost daily I made it a practice to share these morning thoughts on my Facebook page where I have reached 5000 friends. I feel a sincere responsibility as a leader in the church to share these divine thoughts, for I truly believe they communicate the mind of God, which the Spirit of God has downloaded to me.

So I invite you to journey with me as I share "*My Morning Thoughts*" by way of this Devotional Book. It is my prayer that you read *a thought a day* for thirty-one continuous days. By doing so I hope you will be blessed, inspired, edified and equipped thus enabling you to form a habit of thinking divinely!

Now grab your journal and let's begin this divine THOUGHT PROCESS! Be sure to take notes for future reference and be sure to answer the question at the end of each morning thought!

DAY 1

YOU MUST HAVE DISCIPLINE TO BE PRODUCTIVE

I woke up thinking you have to be disciplined to be productive! One day I worked for probably a total of six hours on one teaching to finish what had been previously started and two hours on a message in which I was just starting.

This was a very heavy ministry week for me. It began with preaching on a Sunday evening, teaching Bible Class on Wednesday, teaching a women's class on Thursday, teaching a ministers' class on this Sunday and then preaching and ministering TWICE on the following Sunday!

As well, I don't get to disregard any of my other responsibilities as wife, mother and grandmother OR as a Servant Leader who is an Apostle too. I still had to cook, visit the sick, handle the requests of my daughter, go the PAC meetings at my grand baby's school, run errands, handle household business for my husband, pick up my bonus daughter from school etc. etc. attending to the many matters of the church. Whew.... but because I'm disciplined, I am always productive!

I think the first step to discipline is your realization and acceptance to this:

Ecclesiastes 3:1 "To every thing there is a season, and a time to every purpose under the heaven:"

Secondly, to be productive you must discipline yourself to work within the constraints of something called times and seasons. You must understand you have a specific time frame and a certain season to get things done.

Some things will never get done if you don't learn to work on them in the appropriate, allotted time and within the right season. For instance the farmer does not plant a garden in the heart of the winter when the snow is covering the soil; that's not the right time! Doing things out of season does not contribute to your productivity!

So if you are going to be disciplined for productivity purposes you must train yourself to act or work in accordance to the time and season of a thing and by doing so you will be more productive.

PONDER THIS: What can you do to become more disciplined?

Thoughts of the Morning

Sharon R. Peters

DAY 2

FOLLOW PEACE

I had an early morning wake up where I felt impressed to pray for the mental state of not one person, but many people. I thought, *"Lord, I'm sleeping so good and peaceful right now and you wake me to pray for people who are in mental turmoil right now"?* He did not reply, but I guess if He did answer he'd say *"who is better equipped to pray for them than one who is sober in their mind and one who is resting in peace".* So I awakened and prayed accordingly!

People of God, listen to the scriptures...

Romans 14:19 "Let us therefore follow after the things which make for peace, and things wherewith one may edify another."

Stop, and I repeat stop, following non-peaceful people, stop being in war zones where the peace of God does not reside!

Peace is a fruit of the Spirit and when that fruit manifests itself in a person or an environment, then that's a good person to follow or a good place to be!

The opposite of peace is war and often because you are not at peace in your mind this causes you to be in constant war in your thoughts. Therefore, you must make for peace! How do you make for peace? Let me help you!

Forgive!

Let It Go!

Stop Pondering Negativity!

Stop Perpetuating It In Conversation!

Thank God!

Look To Jesus And Not To Man!

PONDER THIS: What can you do to maintain your peace?

_____
_____
_____
_____
_____
_____
_____

Thoughts of the Morning

SHARON R. PETERS

DAY 3

YOUR DAILY WORD

Matthew 6:11 "Give us this day our daily bread."

In my walk with Christ I turn to the scriptures and not to the prophet for my daily word. I realized a long time ago that there is an accompanying word for THIS DAY! I also realized long ago that God provides fresh manna everyday!

I may not get a Rhema or a prophetic word every day from God but manna is provided for me to go and obtain every day from the word of God.

If you study Israel's plights in the Bible while in the wilderness, you will see that God provided the manna, bread from heaven, for them daily, but it was their responsibility to go out and get it for themselves and their family for six days! Then on the sixth day they got to double up on the manna so that they could observe the Sabbath!

Exodus 16:21-22 "And they gathered it every morning, every man according to his eating: and when the sun waxed hot, it melted. And it came to pass, that on the sixth day they gathered twice as much bread, two omers for one man: and all the rulers of the congregation came and told Moses."

Notice what God allowed to happen when the children of Israel tried to save the manna for the next day!

Exodus 16:19-20 "And Moses said, Let no man leave of it till the morning. Notwithstanding they hearkened not unto Moses; but some of them left of it until the morning, and it bred worms, and stank: and Moses was wroth with them."

Now I have to believe there were two reasons for this:

1. God wanted the children to seek out the bread for life daily as their practice
2. He did not want them becoming complacent with eating yesterday's bread

Likewise, I believe God wants us, His children to seek out His word daily to feast on!

PONDER THIS: What is your word or scripture that you picked up for you to accompany THIS DAY?

_____

_____

_____

_____

_____

Thoughts of the Morning

DAY 4

ARE YOU READY?

The old saints would often ask you this *question "Baby would you be ready if Jesus came back today"?* It was their way of witnessing and evangelizing to the lost.

Even the Apostle Paul said he was ready to be offered up, hear the scripture:

2 *Timothy 4:6 "For I am now ready to be offered, and the time of my departure is at hand."*

Yet my question to you is are you ready for the next chapter of your life here on earth?

Everyone wants NEXT, but have you prepared for the NEXT? Or will you just show up unprepared talking about; *"I've arrived"* or *"I'm here"*, but are clueless as to what you are there for.

Although many don't like processes, this is what prepares you for what's NEXT in your life. Processes involve something called time, which is why we say in the process of time, this occurred or that happened!

I thank God that He used time to process me. For it caused me to prepare for my next and by me submitting to the process I did not show up unprepared.

Know this, just because you are invited to your NEXT PLACE does not mean you get to show up unprepared! Just getting to your NEXT should not be your only goal but getting there and being prepared for it should be.

PONDER THIS: What things can you do now to prepare you for your next that will enhance your readiness for it?

_____

_____

_____

_____

_____

_____

_____

_____

_____

Thoughts of the Morning

Sharon R. Peters

DAY 5

HOW COMFORTING ARE YOU?

John 14:18 "I will not leave you comfortless: I will come to you."

No human being wants to be left without some form of comfort while in a distressing time of his or her life! As Jesus was mentally preparing His disciples for His death and His departure from the earth He wanted to assure them that He would not leave them comfortless!

Everyone wants to experience some form of comfort; it goes along with being human. Even God knew that when Jesus went through a hard time with the devil in the wilderness He as a human in the flesh, would need some comfort. See the scriptures:

Matthew 4:11 "Then the devil leaveth him, and, behold, angels came and ministered unto him."

There is an element of ministry that should bring comfort to human beings.

Even prophecy should bring comfort.

1 Corinthians 14:3 "But he that prophesieth speaketh unto men to edification, and exhortation, and comfort."

God is the God of ALL COMFORT!

2 Corinthians 1:3-5 "Blessed be God, even the Father of our Lord Jesus Christ, the Father of mercies, and the God of all comfort; Who comforteth us in all our tribulation, that we may be able to comfort them which are in any trouble, by the comfort wherewith we ourselves are comforted of God. For as the sufferings of Christ abound in us, so our consolation also aboundeth by Christ."

When we are comforted it brings solace with it, which is an alleviation of our distresses or discomfort.

So my friend when you have the ability to comfort, whether it's through your presence, some act of kindness, your touch, your deeds, your words or your ministry in terms of service it's shows two things!

1. That you care and are concerned as a Human Being
2. That as a Spirit Being you are God like in nature

Comfort warms the soul of the person in distress or agony.

PONDER THIS: What can you do to be more comforting to humanity?

Thoughts of the Morning

DAY 6

PAIN FORGOTTEN EQUATES JOY

John 16:21 "A woman when she is in travail hath sorrow, because her hour is come: but as soon as she is delivered of the child, she remembereth no more the anguish, for joy that a man is born into the world."

When you study the Bible you will see that if someone wanted to describe the ultimate pain or the intensity of heightened pain they would liken the pain to a women in travail during childbirth.

THIS IS THE ULTIMATE PAIN! This is heightened or intense pain from a biblical perspective. Not a broken heart, but the pain a woman experiences when she is birthing a child into the world. The anguish of this is horrific and boy do I know this to be true, both naturally and spiritually.

However, what I found most interesting about this and what I also know to be true is that the pain of birthing is a pain that is hard to remember once the baby is born. It is a pain you forget because of the intensity of the joy that follows the birthing.

This really made me ponder and proclaim this statement:

"Pain that you can no longer remember is your sign that you are healed!" YES GLORY TO GOD!

If you now laugh, about what use to make you cry, it's a sign of healing.

Conversely, if you are still talking about how much they hurt you; it means that you can still remember and recall the pain. This is not good! It is a true indication that you are still in need of healing.

As for me, I love NOT remembering my pain! I don't bury pain, but I just can't remember it once I'm healed. I love being PAIN FREE! Every day I wake up free of pain, I know I am healed or I'm delivered of that thing. Bless God, He did it and I allowed him to do it too.

What about you my friend, DO YOU STILL REMEMBER THE PAIN of that infringement, that let down, that betrayal, that incident, that disappointment? If so, ask God, your Father, *"Why do I still remember the pain Lord?"* Ask Him, *"Lord, why have I not entered into Your joy seeing that you delivered me from that painful situation?"* Again, *"Why God am I remembering that pain?"*

My friend could it be that you are refusing to let go of that incident, even though horrific pain is associated to it?

THOUGHTS OF THE MORNING

I COMMAND YOU TO LOOSE IT AND LET PAIN GO NOW AND THAT BY DOING SO YOU WILL REMEMBER IT NO MORE!

Now enter thou into the joy of the Lord!

———————————————

PONDER THIS: How can you turn your pain into something that is useful to mankind?

_____

_____

_____

_____

_____

_____

_____

_____

_____

_____

DAY 7

HAVE YOU HAD A PERSONAL AWAKENING YET?

I awakened this morning feeling like a queen so I went into my prophetic archives and I pulled up a prophetic word that I received from a prophet, almost 2 years ago on 11/20/13.

Allow me to share a portion of the Prophecy~

"Prepare to cover *jurisdictions*. God says, "I have given you the authority to spiritually govern neighborhoods, cities and states...the anointing you bear sits above the chaos that is taking place in the earth realm."

God says, "You bear a queens anointing to the rule of territory. Prepare to uproot, replace and replant people, places and things through the word of God for you have been crowned for this season and the level of work." Rise up and accept the work and the call of the queen over jurisdictions.

Jurisdictional government and rule in the realms of the spirit, is what I have. This is the nature of my crown for this season that has been placed upon me in the earth as it is in the heavens and I have awakened like Tabitha to this. Therefore, on this day it's fixed, I NOW ACCEPT THIS WORK!

Thank you Holy Ghost. I remember years ago walking into a room and a man said to me "Who are you? Are you a Mayor or something?" I replied, "No I'm a preacher." I realize now that man saw my governmental rule, which I had in spirit.

I thank God for the prophets who speak a thing that gives direction and identity before it happens!

Now remember this statement, "It's not in the title, it's in the awakening"!

PONDER THIS: So with this, what new WORK do you think you will be awakened and revived for in this new season in God?

_____
_____
_____
_____
_____
_____
_____
_____

Thoughts of the Morning

DAY 8

I KNOW WHO I AM~ THEREFORE I PLEDGE ACCORDINGLY

I am an heir of God the Father and I am a joint heir with Christ Jesus and you are too, if you are a child of God.

Romans 8:16-17 "The Spirit itself beareth witness with our spirit, that we are the children of God: And if children, then heirs; heirs of God, and joint-heirs with Christ; if so be that we suffer with him, that we may be also glorified together."

Heirs work with the Father; joint heirs serve together, in terms of the Father's will even if we have to suffer.

What we as heirs don't do, is fight against our Father's will.

So I say, God whatever you are doing in this season I am in agreement to your will and you can count me in as a participative player.

I will not sit as a dormant unresponsive player dear Lord, but I will engage in your plans and your purpose as a mature son or heir so that your desired will is done in the earth in this season.

PONDER THIS: Who are you? **Write seven "I AM" statements that define YOU by God's design?**

DAY 9

ARE YOU THE HELP?

While preparing my things and myself this morning I thought on this one word, HELP! As I thought on that word I made a mental note to send a letter before the year-end to those who are assigned and appointed to help me.

Do you know that help is a set gift in the church? Look, for it is:

1 Corinthians 12:28 "And God hath set some in the church, first apostles, secondarily prophets, thirdly teachers, after that miracles, then gifts of healings, (helps), governments, diversities of tongues."

Helps is plural so it should be in abundance in the body, yet you rarely hear people say "I AM THE HELP", but they will tell you they've been sent to you on assignment.

Notice right after the miracle gift, HELP is set.

Look how Ananias helped Brother Saul after his Damascus road experience!

Acts 9:17 "And Ananias went his way, and entered into the house; and putting his hands on him said, Brother Saul, the Lord, even Jesus, that appeared unto thee in the way as thou camest, hath sent me, that thou mightest receive thy sight, and be filled with the Holy Ghost."

Then right before the set gift of government or administration is HELP.

Look how Barnabas helped Paul with his administration as an Apostle in the Lord's church!

Acts 9:26-27 "And when Saul was come to Jerusalem, he assayed to join himself to the disciples: but they were all afraid of him, and believed not that he was a disciple. But Barnabas took him, and brought him to the apostles, and declared unto them how he had seen the Lord in the way, and that he had spoken to him, and how he had preached boldly at Damascus in the name of Jesus."

My question to you is this, ARE YOU THE HELP? I know the world says "good help is hard to find" but this should not be so in the church because God has, already set THE HELP.

Therefore, will THE HELP please manifest yourself and come forth; we need you in greater representation, for you are a gift to the body!

PONDER THIS: Whose help are you and how can you be a BETTER HELP to them?

DAY 10

AND THERE SHALL BE RECOMPENSE

While driving early this morning I just began to thank God then I began praying for my dear sweet friend and co laborer Apostle Nina-Marie.

After praying and as I drove in silence I thought on the justices of God then I heard the word recompense.

Justice is often received through recompense because it repays someone for the wrong they UNJUSTLY suffered or the trouble they endured.

That word RECOMPENSE means this:

To repay; remunerate; reward, as for service, aid, etc. To pay or give compensation for; make restitution or requital for (damage, injury, or the like).

There is a God that ensures our recompense and his name is Jehovah GMOLAH!

Listen to Boaz speaking concerning Ruth in regards to her recompense:

Ruth 2:11-12 "And Boaz answered and said unto her, It hath fully been shewed me, all that thou hast done unto thy mother in law since the death of thine husband: and how thou hast left thy father and thy mother, and the land of thy nativity, and art come unto a people which thou knewest not heretofore." The Lord recompense thy work, and a full reward be given thee of the Lord God of Israel, under whose wings thou art come to trust.

When Jehovah GMOLAH gets involved in your life, He's coming to give you your just reward, your just pay or to give you your due compensation for the deeds or work you've done, good or bad.

For Ruth that meant another husband named Boaz.

In any event, the Lord of Host has enlightened me that recompense, your full reward is coming.

PONDER THIS: What are you willing to let LORD GOD JEHOVAH give you recompense for; go ahead name them one by one!

_____

_____

_____

_____

_____

_____

_____

Thoughts of the Morning

SHARON R. PETERS

DAY 11

SUBMIT TO THE TRAINING

As I was awakened very early this morning I saw a quick vision of me reading the aforementioned words in a book; *"and eat the food of your successful training"*.

Then while I was driving early this morning I kept repeating those words for truly God was personally enlightening me to something, so I had to comprehend it. Therefore, I pondered it as I drove.

Now because I know how God deals with me in utterances, I knew this sighting was one, letting me know I had successfully passed my test and two, that the current process that I had to submit myself to out of obedience to God's will was actually some kind of training for me. It had availed me or had caused the production of a particular food or we can say result that I could now personally partake in! WOW!!!!!

My process, which involved training was in essence producing a type of divine tailor made harvest for me that I could personally eat from.

What started out as a bitter cup that I had to drink, if I was going to remain in God's will had now turned to food or a result that I could now partake in and gladly eat from!

I was going from drinking something bitter to now being allowed to eat some good food!

Jesus said it like this in the scriptures:

John 4:34 "Jesus saith unto them, My "meat" (sustenance) is to do the will of him that sent me, and to finish his work. "

It's as if I can hear God saying, "C'mon Sharon go ahead TASTE AND SEE that I am GOOD!"

What's good is His will!

What's good is when you submit to His processes that will mature you to finish His work, which He has assigned for you to complete.

What's good is His processes of life will cause you to produce His desired fruit that you can enjoy.

Truly this gives new meaning to the scripture: *Psalm 34:8 "O taste and see that the Lord is good: blessed is the man that trusteth in him."*

Remember this:

You have to trust the process that takes you into the goodness of the Lord.

Now I can truly say as a leader, I've tasted and seen for myself that the Lord is good.

I leave you with this, SUBMIT TO THE TRAINING, which is often wrapped up in your process to greater, because it's some good stuff in there that you will be glad to partake in, in its finished results!

P.S. You may not like where you are now in your process but Stay Tuned, MORE IS COMING, if you submit to the training.

PONDER THIS: What of God's will do you need to submit to though it be likened unto a bitter cup?

_____
_____
_____
_____
_____
_____
_____
_____

THOUGHTS OF THE MORNING

DAY 12

Don't Say It

So often our current situation tries to force us to say, decree and declare something that is temporal and have nothing to do with the eternal plan of God for our life.

Yes temporal situations and occurrences are often what we see with our natural eyes, but our faith can show us things in another realm that cannot be seen with the natural eye.

It is those unseen things that we must use our faith to speak on, decree and declare. We must allow our faith, coupled with the right words spoken about what is unseen to shape a new world for us beyond our current situation. Hear the word:

Hebrews 11:3 "Through faith we understand that the worlds were framed by the word of God, so that things which are seen were not made of things which do appear."

So when you see something naturally, that does not line up with your faith, DON'T SAY IT! WHY? Because it's temporal and it's going to change and you don't want to have to eat the fruit of those words.

When you see something naturally that does not look

like what God promised you in His word, DON'T SAY IT! Remember God is not slack concerning His promises so if what you see is contrary to your promise, then it's only temporal!

Again, don't say or proclaim any temporal situation as the end all or be all for your life because IT IS NOT!

You must know and believe that God has some eternal goodness for you so DON'T say anything contrary to God's word!

Learn to blink at temporal situations of life and seek to see your promise by faith because that's eternal.

PONDER THIS: What can you do to rehab your speech?

_____

_____

_____

_____

_____

_____

Special thanks to my daughter Elder Damietta Jeffries a teacher in the Body of Christ for our speech rehab classes at the church, it helped us speak more in line with the word of God!

DAY 13

DO YOU REALLY KNOW YOUR DESIGNATION?

When I awakened this morning as I opened my eyes I heard these words in my spirit "learning is knowing".

I always seek to match my revelatory hearings with the logos or the written word of God. Therefore, upon hearing this morning's download I immediately thought of Jesus and what the scripture says He, the Lord, learned!

Hebrews 5:8-10 "Even though Jesus was the Son of God or a son; with all the rights and privileges of an heir, (he learned obedience) by what he suffered through "total obedience" to God, Jesus achieved the glorified or perfected state God originally intended for human beings;"

And because "his obedience was perfect" or having achieved perfection, he was able to give became the source/means of eternal salvation to all who obey him. In this way God made designated; appointed Jesus a high priest, a priest like in the priestly order/line of Melchizedek;

Now understand this, Jesus was never disobedient as a son, however the sufferings that he endured caused Him to be perfected or complete in His obedience all the way to the cross which held his complete purpose.

Jesus' sufferings caused him to learn what total obedience to God could avail him as His son! Jesus learned and now knows as He sits on the right hand of the Father that total obedience to God brings an appointment and a high level of glory to God himself!

Jesus reached his highest designation because his learning caused him to really know His rightful place in God. This is powerful because Jesus' total obedience not only led him to his destination, but it caused him to know his true designation, i.e. nomination, appointment or election.

Likewise, it is through your learning that you come to know the totality of your purpose, your calling, nominations, election, appointments etc. Your learning confirms your knowing in your spirit as certain manifestations await you.

If you don't allow divine learning experiences to have the proper place in your life there will be so much you will never know.

So as I submit to this higher learning, which has been divinely appointed to me, I'm trusting God that I will have a higher definition of my life and I will truly know my designation in Him!

PONDER THIS: WHO ARE YOU BY GOD'S DESIGN?

Thoughts of the Morning

DAY 14

THE STRENGTH OF THE EAGLES WINGS

As I awakened feeling tired and still battling a headache from the day before I heard these words in my spirit ~

The strength of the eagles' wings and of course I know the scripture in *Isaiah 40:28-31* which says:

Hast thou not known? Hast thou not heard, that the (everlasting God), the Lord, the Creator of the ends of the earth, fainteth not, neither is weary? There is no searching of his understanding. He giveth power to the faint; and to them that have no might he increaseth strength. Even the youths shall faint and be weary, and the young men shall utterly fall:

But they that wait upon the Lord shall renew their strength; they shall mount up with "wings as eagles"; they shall run, and not be weary; and they shall walk, and not faint.

Yet I felt God wanted me to go deeper so I researched the strength of the Eagles' wing and made a revelatory discovery that will really bless you!

LOOK AT THIS:

The eagle has the longest life span of its species. It

can live up to 70 years, but to reach this age, the eagle must make a hard decision. In its 40's its long and flexible talons (claws) can no longer grab prey, which serves as food. Its long and sharp beak becomes bent. Its old-aged and heavy wings, due to their thick feathers, become stuck to its chest and make it difficult to fly. So the eagle is left with only two options: die or go through a painful process of change, which lasts 150 days.

The process to maturity we can say requires that the eagle fly to a mountaintop and sit on its nest. There the eagle knocks its beak against a rock until it plucks it out. After plucking it out, the eagle will wait for a new beak to grow back and then it will pluck out its talons (claws). When its new talons grow back, the eagle starts plucking its old-aged feathers. And after five months, the eagle takes its famous flight of rebirth and lives for 30 more years.

This is the process of rebirth that an eagle must endure to mount up with renewed strength in his wings!

This is also the process of maturity that an eagle must go through to take its famous flight. We can also say the extended life of an eagle is in the process of his rebirth. If he can submit to this painful process he can live and soar another 30 years. WOW! Good God from Zion!

So when God tells us, who have become tired and weary, that we are going to mount up with wings as eagles, remember the strength of the eagle's wings was born from a grueling process that he submitted to up on his nest in the mountain (on a rock)!

I think by now you can see where I'm going with this, so go ahead child of God, GO TO THE ROCK AND COMPLETE YOUR PROCESS!

PONDER THIS: What divine processes are you currently enduring that are working strength in you for the journey? Write about how it's making you stronger!

_____
_____
_____
_____
_____
_____
_____
_____

Thoughts of the Morning

DAY 15

THE KINGDOM UNIT

It's an awesome thing when men and women can work harmoniously together for kingdom purposes, void of gender prejudices!

Our ministerial efforts become more attractive universally when we present ourselves as a unit. Our tribes are strengthened and fortified when they have a unit in front of them. We are more structurally sound as a unit. The enemy is often rebuked when he sees a man/woman unit.

In addition, when both genders are showcased in kingdom efforts it removes bias and stereotypes of inequality. Of course we understand that there are times and occasions for specific ministry for a certain sect of people, however our general kingdom work should exhibit men and women working together with equal efforts.

Even our children should be permitted to join us as we make kingdom statements by our presence in the earth.

The days of discussions about can a woman do this and can a woman do that should really be extinct by now for truly women have proven we can gracefully carry not only the word but also the oil. We too as women can be Kingdom leaders without obstructing the order of God as it relates to the God given leadership order of the man. We understand this as women and the majority of us have no problem with it. As well we also understand that we were included in divine kingdom assignments.

As I travel and observe kingdom at work, I see that many men and women of God do understand Kingdom equality and those that do are having great ministry success and are being used by God to do greater! They have truly become a force of unity to be reckoned with.

So I say to those that get this, please continue together for I truly believe that God will be joining and uniting more men and women of God for Kingdom purposes, for truly two is better than one.

PONDER THIS: Name someone of the opposite sex who you can partner with for a kingdom purpose and write a proposal that you may present to that person to fulfill a common cause!

_____

_____

Thoughts of the Morning

DAY 16

SIT IN A PLACE OF PREPARATION

As I meditated one morning, I began to discern that I was sitting in a place of preparation. I thought to myself what does that mean?

Then my mind recalled another time in the natural, where I sat in a place of preparation. It was in the nursery that I had prepared for my grandchild who made her arrival into the earth five years ago.

For months I transformed a room in my home to a baby's room. I painted, put up wallpaper, brought in baby furniture, put the new clothes in her closet and in her dresser. Filled the changing table with diapers etc.

Then when the room was completely finished and filled with everything my new grand baby would need, I found myself coming into that room everyday and just sat in that room. I would pray, worship and sing songs of praise and thanksgiving in that room. I would bless God for her right there in the room, which was prepared in advance for her.

I SAT IN A PLACE OF PREPARATION!

Although our new bundle of joy had not arrived and

as a matter of fact she was still in the womb, I had so much anticipation of her arrival that I was so elated to just sit in the place that had been prepared for her. Can someone catch this?

Well God said in his word in *Luke 14:17 "Come all things are ready NOW"*!

There is a prepared place where I can sit now! You don't have to sit in places called defeat or despair trying to anticipate from that place, trying to hope from that place; IT AIN'T GONNA HAPPEN!

God wants us sitting in places that have been prepared for us and that is in heavenly places with Christ Jesus, which is a place of VICTORY AND DOMINION that is already prepared. It's a spiritual place where earthly woes can't alter life by God's design.

People of God mount up to your prepared place in the realms of the spirit and sit there as you anticipate the promises of God from that place. The view from that place is so much more encouraging and the wait from that place is so comforting!

PONDER THIS: What or (who) is God preparing you for?

Thoughts of the Morning

DAY 17

WRONG EXPERIENCE ~ RIGHT REASON

I have been hearing these words in my spirit off and on repeatedly! I knew God was speaking to me as to reveal His plans for me!

I heard Him say, "I will permit the wrong experience for the right reason"

Well one morning I awakened again with this utterance in my spirit during my sleep time communing with God, which I often have.

At first I kept wondering, Lord what is the wrong experience? Then my mind quickly pondered, WHAT IS THE RIGHT REASON? For that seemed more important to me than the wrong experience.

The pit for Joseph was wrong yet; his being in it was so right!

The fiery furnace was so wrong for the three Hebrew boys but it was for the right reason they were thrown in.

The lion's den was so wrong for Daniel to be put in but it was so right for him to be there.

Job's entire experience was so wrong and so painful

psychologically, emotionally and physically but the reason for all of this was so right!

It was so wrong for Lazarus to have to get sick and die then lie in a tomb for days, but it was for the right reason!

Even the cross that Jesus had to endure by suffering and dying on was so wrong for him to have to experience, but look at all the right reasons for his death by crucifixion.

Again I say unto you; God will permit the wrong experience for the right reason! So you must have extreme trust in Him, being assured that something right will come out of the divine wrong experience. You must move past from the hurtful horrific experience and seek to know the right reason(s) for it because there is one, maybe even more!

Lastly, one thing I saw in common with all the aforementioned wrong experiences was this: THEY WERE ALL ELEVATED OR EXALTED BY GOD ALMIGHTY IN SOME WAY!

PONDER THIS: What were some of the right places that the wrong experiences landed you? Think about it and right them down and give God praise for his infinite wisdom and ordained providence over your life!

_____

_____

_____

_____

_____

_____

_____

_____

_____

_____

_____

_____

_____

_____

_____

_____

Thoughts of the Morning

DAY 18

YOU MUST ACKNOWLEDGE CHANGE

I was cooking some breakfast for my husband and as I stood over the bacon as it was frying up in the pan, I began to notice how the appearance of the bacon was changing right before my eyes as it endured the heat. See I like watching over my bacon as I cook it because it allows me to know the precise moment when to "flip it" so as not to overlook it or burn it.

I'm going somewhere with this analogy, just stay with me it's going to bless you and make you think too, maybe even repent.

As I stood there watching over my bacon and flipping it, I witnessed the bacon change to a golden pleasing brown, which we both love!

I then thought, how often we as people fail to recognize when someone or the matter that we have interceded about has changed!

How often do we celebrate or congratulate others for their change?

We certainly talked about them when they were in that un-desirous state of being but when we see change in them, why don't we acknowledge it and celebrate them accordingly, especially since you hoped and prayed for it.

Why does change go so unnoticed?

As people who watch over souls why don't we tell those we watch over these comforting words, "Sweetheart I see you are changing", then celebrate them accordingly. We are quick to put down the unchanged soul so why don't we uplift and encourage the soul that is changing? Or is it that we have eyes that don't really see through the eyes of God? The moment God detects change of heart He lifts the sentence.

We must really do better because I can hear God saying it's time to flip the script for the manifestation of change is here, so let's rejoice and celebrate the beautiful butterfly for she has evolved through change.

PONDER THIS: What about you or a family member has changed that you failed to recognize or even acknowledge?

_____

_____

THOUGHTS OF THE MORNING

DAY 19

STOP IT!

There are some things you've got to stop doing in this new season of your life!

Like:

STOP seeking and sharing non-edifying information on social media!

STOP requiring so much personal attention and PAY ATTENTION!

STOP being so gullible and develop some influence of your own!

STOP being so devil focused and start being more GOD CONSCIOUS so that you can ignite spiritual awareness!

STOP going backward and proceed with caution!

STOP losing momentum but keep up!

STOP rehashing old stuff and bringing up the past just focus on the new!

STOP LYING and tell the truth!

STOP being carnal and practice being spiritual!

STOP it with the hater thoughts and mentality and go ahead and show yourself friendly!

STOP being so fearful and allow yourself to be loved so that you can learn to love!

STOP putting yourself and others down; learn to build up!

STOP playing games and grow up!

STOP whining and start winning!

STOP meandering in the valley and make the climb to the mountain!

STOP rehearsing your wounds and get healed for good!

STOP refusing to forgive and let it go!

STOP taking yourself so serious and lose the pompous attitude!

STOP being a hell raiser and seek to be a peacemaker!

And Finally,

STOP doubting God and trust in him with your whole heart for GREAT THINGS AWAIT US!

PONDER THIS: It's a new day what do you need to stop and what can you start doing?

Thoughts of the Morning

DAY 20

UN-COMPLICATE YOUR LIFE

God shows me a lot by way of dreams and visions. I dream almost every night and have for years.

I recall a dream I hade when I was walking through my old house and a host of my spiritual children were there, my natural children and some of their friends. As well as my bonus children which I acquired through marriage were following me around the house, one of which I was carrying as I walked through this very cluttered house. I mean stuff was everywhere, out of order and in disarray. I got *madder* (that's not a word I know) with every step I took. I continued to say, "How can you all live like this." In addition, I was wondering why no one else in the house seemed bothered. Everyone was just busy doing whatever he or she was doing. I woke up mad!

And as I lay there thinking of this dream I thought Lord we make life so complicated. We entangle our life with stuff that has nothing to do with life.

Life by God's design is not cluttered neither is it complicated. Life is simply breath. See the word.

"And the Lord God formed man of the dust of the ground,

and breathed into his nostrils the (breath of life); and man became a living soul." Genesis 2:7

Life is not a car, a dress, a ministry, a boyfriend or a chick on the side! Life is not the acquisition of a bunch of stuff either!

LIFE IS BREATH that comes from God. The end.

And *2 Peter 1:3* lets us know this:

"According as his divine power hath given unto us all things that pertain unto (life) and godliness, through the knowledge of him that hath called us to glory and virtue: "

So anything that we need that pertain to life, God himself has already given us those things and I promise you those things are in the kingdom just as the tree of life was in the garden of Eden. This is why he told us in *Matthew 6:33* to seek the kingdom first!

Therefore, people of God please un-complicate your life! Keep it simple for as long as you have the breath of God and are not sucking up the air released by the Prince of this world. You have a good life, so seek now to live the life abundantly that Jesus came for you to have!

As for me, I'm LIVING THE GOOD LIFE IN HD!

PONDER THIS: What can you do to live a life that demonstrates Christ?

_____
_____
_____
_____
_____
_____
_____
_____
_____
_____
_____
_____
_____
_____
_____

Thoughts of the Morning

_____
_____
_____
_____
_____
_____
_____
_____
_____
_____

DAY 21

THE AMAZING SECOND DAY CREATION OF ELOHIM

Now today's thought will truly be a teaching you have probably never heard before so brace yourself!

I woke up laughing because I saw the faces of my Bible Class students last night when I told them as a sidebar lesson that:

"We here on the earth are in between two waters. Meaning there is water above our heads and water below us."

That's when they looked at me like Apostle Sharon goes too far. However, creation shows us this you just have to pay attention to scripture, I'll explain it.

Before the creation of the heavens, not referring to where God lives but the other heavens, and the earth, all there was an abyss.

Genesis 1:1-2 (AMP) "In the beginning God Elohim created by forming from nothing the heavens and the earth. The earth was formless and void or a waste and emptiness, and darkness was upon the face of the deep primeval ocean that covered the unformed earth. The Spirit of God was moving hovering, brooding over the face of the waters."

I was trying to explain to my class that when you think of Hell or the grave, think beyond the cemetery or six feet under, think of it being the abyss or below sea level or in the inner most lowest infernal region of the earth.

Then I mentioned the earth being positioned between waters was when God separated the waters from the waters and then put a firmament (or the vault of heaven, the sky) in between the waters, see the scriptures because this was an amazing second day creation.

Genesis 1:6-10 "And God said, Let there be a firmament (or a sky) in the midst of the waters, and let it "divide the waters from the waters".

So you see the sky hides the water that is above your head. AMAZING! Let's continue.

And God made the firmament, and divided the waters, which were under the firmament from the waters, which were above the firmament: and it was so. (Read this again)

So water is ABOVE AND BENEATH THE EARTH!

Let's continue.

And God called the firmament Heaven. And the evening and the morning were the second day.

And God said, Let the waters (under the heaven) be gathered together unto one place, and let the dry land appear: and it was so.

The appearance of dry land or EARTH came into existence simply because God (Elohim) gathered the water that was under the heaven into one place to cause an appearance of something that he would call into existence and that was the creation of the earth.

See the WORD:

And God called the dry land Earth; and the gathering together of the waters called he Seas: and God saw that it was good.

Then the water He gathered He changed its name to seas and so there you have it.

And you doubt that God can pay your bills, save your wayward son or change the heart of your husband!

Elohim is a *BAD GOD*; He divides water from water and makes an earth! Whew now wrap your mind around that and all this started simply with the Spirit moving and God saying LET THERE BE!

PONDER THIS: What unlimited resources of God might you tap into if you learned how to say LET THERE BE in faith?

THOUGHTS OF THE MORNING

DAY 22

Are You Comfortable?

One night I had a very short dream that gave me a great sense of resolve.

In the dream I was laying on the floor shivering in what looked like my bedroom. I was so cold. Then this man came over to me with a big warm comforter and He covered me and immediately I was no longer cold. I immediately stopped shaking. The blanket felt so cozy and warm. As the man put the blanket over me He said to me; "You've got to be taught how to be comfortable." Then I woke up!

In my waking, I had such a good feeling about this dream. I mean it gave me such comfort and I pondered it so as to interpret it, which I'm gifted to interpret dreams.

Allow me to interpret my dream for you.

Lying on the floor in my bedroom symbolizes a condition of living.

Shivering, while lying on the floor symbolizes some unfavorable condition of life in terms of having what is needed to make one comfortable.

The man covering me with the blanket symbolizes the Lord, covering me with that which I needed, making me quite comfortable in life.

The man's or THE LORD'S words "you've got to be taught how to be comfortable" speaks of me learning how to live in a more than adequate or a more sufficient state of being like in prosperity.

What I noticed in the dream was that I did not get off the floor I remained there covered and sufficiently provided for. I WAS COMFORTABLE! This made me think of this scripture or the words of David!

Psalm 30:5-6 ...weeping may endure for a night, but joy cometh in the morning. And in my prosperity I said, I shall never be moved.

This is an awesome dream, which is why I felt so good when I awakened. It even gave me confirmation to get my bills in order and ready to be paid.

So I want to ask you today, are you ready to be comfortable? Are you, people of God, ready to live comfortably in prosperity as kingdom citizens?

God knows I am! God is about to make me comfortable and He's gonna teach me how to live in that level of prosperity! GLORY TO GOD!

PONDER THIS: What can you do to prepare for great prosperity and go beyond money?

DAY 23

HOW POISED ARE YOU?

I woke up one morning with one word in my spirit and that word was poise. I thought okay God where are we going with this word this morning? Lord, what do you want me to see and share. So I looked up this familiar word in the dictionary although I associated "poise" kinda to posture or a type "graceful presentation" of one's self!

However I saw something more! Allow me to share~

The definition of poise is:

A state of balance or equilibrium, as from equality or equal distribution of weight. A dignified, self-confident manner or composure.

However these last two definitions really caught my attention and I was beginning to see and understand what the Lord was showing me.

Poise is a type of suspense or wavering, as between rest and motion. Poise is the state or position of hovering like the poise of a bird in the air.

Revelatory Speaking~ Poise is likened unto the character and workings of the Holy Spirit in the life of the believer.

It is the Spirit of God that takes you from a place of rest to motion.

Remember it was the Spirit of God that hovered over the abyss (i.e. those dark waters)! Hear the Word:

Genesis 1:2 (AMP) "The earth was without form and an empty waste, and darkness was upon the face of the very great deep. The Spirit of God was moving hovering, brooding over the face of the waters."

Likewise, it is that same Spirit that is poised or hovering over those dark uncreated or unshaped places in your life, which allows you to simply rest as the Spirit decides when to move so creation can begin! And remember creation is according to God's word! Simply LET THERE BE~

In addition, it is the Spirit being poised in the life of the believer that makes them CONFIDENT!

It is the Spirit of God being operational and poised in your life that is balancing the weights of life and that balance is giving you a sense of composure!

Therefore no *freak-out* sessions are needed as long as the Spirit of God is poised in your life!

So as you go through your day today remember this one word, POISE and simply REST in HIM who you live, move and have your being!

PONDER THIS: How can you perfect your poise during times of trouble?

DAY 24

DO YOU HAVE THE MINISTRY OF RECONCILIATION?

I had another early morning start to my day and as I was driving I began praying! As I prayed with my intellect addressing my concerns to God, the Spirit began to help me pray better and I found myself interceding for those saints that needed to be reconciled with another saint of God.

I began to think about how it seems so difficult for saints of the Most High God to reconcile with each other when there is an ought or a transgression that separates them. I said, "God how can this be when you said in your word that you have given us your people the ministry of reconciliation.

2 Corinthians 5:17-19 "Therefore if any man be in Christ, he is a new creature: old things are passed away; behold, all things are become new. And all things are of God, who hath reconciled us to himself by Jesus Christ, and hath given to us the ministry of reconciliation; To wit, that God was in Christ, reconciling the world unto himself, not imputing their trespasses unto them; and hath committed unto us the (word of reconciliation)."

Now we know ministry in and of itself is a work, so

we've been given a job that entails helping the world be reconciled back to God. However, how can we reconcile a people who don't know their God back to Him when we can't even be reconciled with our own brother or sister in Christ? I must admit I'm perplexed as to why this ministry is not operable within the church. What's hindering our reconciliation with each other as believers?

- Is it our unwillingness to forgive?
- Is it our unwillingness to forget?
- Is it our stubbornness of our pride?
- Is it our need to punish one another for wrong done?
- Is it the hardness of our heart?
- Is it the fear of being let down or done wrong again?
- Is it that we reach a point of finality with each other and we say "enough is enough" and too much is TOO MUCH?

Or is it ALL OF THE ABOVE and more?

Whatever it is I can assure you that if we cannot activate the ministry of reconciliation within the church then we will never be able to reconcile a sinner back to God.

So let me try to help you better serve in this ministry by defining it?

WHAT DOES IT MEAN TO RECONCILE?

It means simply TO MAKE PEACE! Not make for peace, that's pretend and phony, but to actually MAKE PEACE!

It means to be in harmony or in agreement again.

It means to settle a dispute, quarrel or argument.

It means to WIN OVER TO FRIENDLINESS!

It means to cause to be amicable again.

And here's a spiritual definition I hear in my spirit for RECONCILIATION~

When you reconcile with someone you reinstitute the goodwill of God back into the relationship.

So I say to you all that are at odds with one another, go ahead and defy the odds and put God's good will back into rotation by being reconciled with your brother or your sister.

And please be RECONCILED with those God ordained leaders/mentors that have been willed by God to get you to your next place in Him!

I'll be praying for you and remember this reconciliation can often happen with "A WORD"! Meaning there is something that you my friend can say that will birth the ministry of reconciliation into the relationship.

So I beseech you my friend to seek the Lord for that word of reconciliation and then go to that person and release that word instead of all those other words that separate and divide.

PONDER THIS: Whom do you need to reconcile with? Write a letter of reconciliation to them and pray about mailing it to them.

Thoughts of the Morning

DAY 25

ARE YOU FRUITFUL?

The extreme opposite of fruitful is barren. However, when you are fruitful you are producing good results, what you are bringing forth is beneficial and profitable to yourself and others. This is one of God's first blessings spoken over mankind in the beginning. BE FRUITFUL...

Even under adverse conditions of life, God wants you to BE FRUITFUL! God never wanted us to toil in life and still bring forth nothing! Joseph, who had a rough life, as a dreamer, from the age of 17 to 30 was still a very fruitful and prosperous young man. Although he was afflicted, Joseph could still produce because God was with him.

Listen to the meaning of Joseph two sons' names:

Genesis 41:51-52 "And Joseph called the name of the firstborn Manasseh: For God, said he, hath made me forget all my toil, and all my father's house. And the name of the second called he Ephraim: For God hath caused me to be fruitful in the land of my affliction".

Fruitfulness will make you forget the experience of your toil. However, you cannot be fruitful in life without the help of God! See, even though Joseph was afflicted in various places in life, God was always with Joseph, so he remained FRUITFUL even in his afflictions!

Now please don't confuse excess with fruitfulness. You can have excess or a lot of stuff without God but you CANNOT be fruitful without the Lord! Let me say that again, YOU CANNOT BE FRUITFUL WITHOUT GOD or the blessing of FRUITFULNESS cannot be on your life without the Lord! I hope you get this.

Remember Peter toiled all night and caught nothing until Jesus told him to launch out into the deep! Jesus made Peter's business FRUITFUL!

Then hear the words of Jesus as written by *John 15:4-5*

"Abide in me, and I in you. As the branch cannot "bear fruit" of itself, except it abide in the vine; no more can ye, except ye abide in me. I am the vine, ye are the branches: He that abideth in me, and I in him, the same "bringeth forth much fruit": for without me ye can do nothing."

The Lord Jesus Christ is the one that makes us fruitful for he is the one that put the blessing of fruitfulness back on our lives!

Fruitfulness is a benefit of your personal salvation plan and that's a good place to praise the Lord!

So people of God it is in your FRUITFULNESS that

you shall multiply!

Lastly, if you are in a place of unfruitfulness or barrenness, check your connectivity to the vine, perhaps you have fallen away or perhaps you have dipped too low or have become bent away from that which you should become connected to! Ask the Lord to raise you up again so that you may once again BE FRUITFUL!

Stay connected to Jesus good people and you shall be fruitful!

PONDER THIS: What area of your life are you lacking in fruitfulness?

_____
_____
_____
_____
_____
_____
_____
_____
_____

Thoughts of the Morning

DAY 26

GOD CARES FOR YOU

EL-ROI, the God that sees YOU and the God that wants you to know that HE cares for you when you are in afflicted states of being was also the God that informed Hagar in the wilderness that she was pregnant.

Let's look at this in *Genesis 16:11 EXB*

"The angel messenger added, "You are now pregnant have conceived, and you will have give birth to a son. You will name him Ishmael sounds like the verb "to hear", because the Lord has heard your cries of your affliction."

Yes EL-ROI is the God that sees YOU in your afflictions, but He is also the God that hears the cries associated with your affliction.

EL-ROI is the God who will reveal to you what you have "conceived" AND what you shall deliver.

Note: Keep in mind that your afflictions are causing you to get pregnant with God's planned increase for your life. I know you never imaged birthing your own increase through your afflictions, but look at the word of God:

Exodus 1:11-12 "Therefore they did set over them taskmasters to afflict them with their burdens. And they built for Pharaoh treasure cities, Pithom and Raamses."

The more they afflicted them, the more they multiplied and grew and they were grieved because of the children of Israel.

PONDER THIS: Name the areas of your life where you need God to deliver you from?

_____
_____
_____
_____
_____
_____
_____
_____
_____
_____
_____
_____

DAY 27

PURIFICATION BEFORE PRESENTATION

All while I slept, for the few hours I got to sleep, I could hear God saying in my spirit "purification before presentation"!

When I awakened Esther came to my mind because I knew she was a woman who had to go through a purification process before she was presented to the king. See the word~

Esther 2:12-13 "Now when every maid's turn was come to go in to king Ahasuerus, (after) that she had been twelve months, according to the manner of the women, for so were the days of their purifications accomplished, to wit, six months with oil of myrrh, and six months with sweet odours, and with other things for the purifying of the women; Then thus came every maiden unto the king; whatsoever she desired was given her to go with her out of the house of the women unto the king's house."

A season of purification must be accomplished in your life before you will receive divine favor from the king, which you will need, in order to execute your kingdom assignment with precision.

Keep in mind that Esther already had favor with man, Hegai, who gave her the things she needed to begin this process of purification, but she didn't have favor with the king yet. Look at the word~

Esther 2:9 "And the maiden pleased him, (Hegai) and she obtained kindness of him; and he speedily gave her her things for purification, with such things as belonged to her, and seven maidens, which were meet to be given her, out of the king's house: and he preferred her and her maids unto the best place of the house of the women."

Now God would have me to tell you don't confuse **purification** with **consecration** for the former comes before the latter.

Purification involves this:

- to make pure; free from anything that debases, pollutes, adulterates, or contaminates:
- to free from foreign, extraneous, or objectionable elements:
- To free from guilt or evil.
- To clear or purge
- To make clean for ceremonial or ritual use.

Consecration involves this:

- To make or declare sacred; set apart or dedicate to the service of a deity
- To make (something) an object of honor or veneration; hallow: a custom consecrated by time.

- To devote or dedicate to some purpose:
- To admit or ordain to a sacred office, especially to the episcopate.

So you see to purify oneself is not the same as consecrating oneself! Purification comes before consecration! Selah

Esther had to purify herself for kingly presentation BEFORE she could consecrate herself for her kingdom purpose, for such a time as this. See the word~

Esther 4:16 "Go, gather together all the Jews that are present in Shushan, and fast ye for me, and neither eat nor drink three days, night or day: I also and my maidens will fast likewise; and so will I go in unto the king, which is not according to the law: and if I perish, I perish."

What am I saying, you may ask?

Before you are fully prepared to execute with precision, your kingdom assignment, you must go through a season of purification that will make you worthy for kingly presentation to God; causing you to obtain divine favor with Him. This will cause you to willingly consecrate yourself for the serving of the Lord's purpose. Thus making you ready to execute your kingdom assignment with strategies from on high!

So I say to you, LET THE PROCESS OF PURIFICATION begin in your life and watch the

Kings and Priestly anointing be poured upon you!

P.S. That's some rich oil too!

PONDER THIS: How may the Lord purify you, what areas of your triune being needs purification?

Thoughts of the Morning

DAY 28

DON'T BE BLIND SIGHTED WITH COMPROMISE

While praying one morning I fell back to sleep and while sleeping I saw a vision of a heavy set woman who was weeping over the possible violence her son could be involved in. Nothing that the woman feared for her son had happened but she was imagining and weeping like it had happened while she was mourning the possible loss of a son she still had.

When I awakened I just laid there awaiting the Lord's leading for my scripture meditation because I knew He was trying to show me something!

The Spirit of the Lord then brought something back to my remembrance that I studied and taught in depth in past years, that was a heathen king in the Old Testament by the name of King Agag, King of the Amalekites. He was the king that Saul spared. He was the King that the Prophet Samuel had to behead. He was the king of the people who were the first enemy to attack the children of Israel while they were in the wilderness.

It was Amalek that showed up to fight with the children of Israel when they were on their way to their promise land so as to cut them off from their destiny and this was an abomination to God according to *Deut 25:16*. It was at a time that God's chosen people weren't even supposed to be fighting yet.

Moses had to fight Amalek on the mountain with the rod of God in his hand with his hands lifted up and Joshua had to fight Amalek in valley in order to confuse or frustrate his plans. *Exodus 17*. God wanted this recorded so he told Moses to put this invasion by this enemy in a memorial book so Joshua, the up and coming leader, would remember this.

LEADER DO NOT COMPROMISE, that's an abomination to me, says the Lord! I don't like unjust measures; I don't like unrighteous measures. I want an end to this from under the heavens; this is not a good representation of the kingdom, which exemplifies justice! See the word correlation here!

Deuteronomy 25:15-19 But thou shalt have a perfect and just weight, a perfect and just measure shalt thou have: that thy days may be lengthened in the land which the Lord thy God giveth thee. For all that do such things, and all that do unrighteously, are an abomination unto the Lord thy God. (Remember what Amalek did unto thee) by the way, when ye were come forth out of Egypt; How he met thee by the way, and smote the hindmost of thee, even all that were feeble behind thee, when thou wast faint and weary; and he feared not God. Therefore it shall be, when the Lord thy God hath given thee rest from all thine enemies round about, in the land which the Lord thy God giveth thee for an inheritance to possess it, that thou shalt blot out the remembrance of Amalek from under heaven; thou shalt not forget it.

So Saul's first assignment as the first king of the children of Israel was to utterly destroy the Amalekites; but he did not do it! He took his assignment too lightly, he feared people more than he revered God's orders and he spared the king of compromise, AGAG. Saul was blindsided! He seemed to not realize the importance of this divine assignment to kill them all. So the prophet had to go after the king himself!

1 Samuel 15:32-33 "Then said Samuel, Bring ye hither to me Agag the king of the Amalekites. And Agag came unto him delicately. And Agag said, Surely the bitterness of death is past. And Samuel said, "As thy sword hath made women childless", so shall thy mother be childless among women. And Samuel hewed Agag in pieces before the Lord in Gilgal."

People of God, it is now the spirit of AGAG, "THE KING OF COMPROMISE" that's killing our children. That murdering spirit is causing grief to mothers everywhere, not just in my city Chicago, where I live.

So you can keep looking at stats and calling us who

live in Chicago, "Chiraq", and "murder capital" if you want, but the real problem is a spiritual one and Agag's head must be cut off. However this time it must be done in the spirit BECAUSE HE IS AN ABOMINATION TO GOD and those who perpetuate the spirit of compromise will lose their kingdom authority if they are part of the Body of Christ!

You cannot compromise the faith!

―――――――――

PONDER THIS: Think about it, where in your life have you compromised in the faith? Once you've identified that area of compromise REPENT NOW!

―――――――――――――――――
―――――――――――――――――
―――――――――――――――――
―――――――――――――――――
―――――――――――――――――
―――――――――――――――――
―――――――――――――――――
―――――――――――――――――
―――――――――――――――――
―――――――――――――――――

DAY 29

HAVE YOU EXPERIENCED LOVE IN OPTIMIZATION?

One of the most awesome love affairs that I have ever experienced as a woman is the love of Christ, which according to Paul surpasses the mere knowledge of Him. It is that experience with Him that has caused me to be used as an instrument of God's love in the earth. Loving others is no longer difficult for me. Loving is automatic for me now. Because of this love affair, I am no longer tormented by fear because love in perfection cast out fear and all manner of insecurities went with it.

This LOVE experience is one that the Apostle Paul prayed for the church in Ephesus to have.

Ephesians 3:14, 17-19 "For this cause I bow my knees unto the Father of our Lord Jesus Christ, That Christ may dwell in your hearts by faith; that ye, being rooted and grounded in love, May be able to comprehend with all saints what is the breadth, and length, and depth, and height; And to know the love of Christ, which passeth knowledge, that ye might be filled with all the fullness of God."

Their apostle knew that if the church was ever going to have relational comprehension with other saints they would have to have a personal love affair with Christ FIRST! Do not think that loving another correctly is an automatic because it is not. However, Jesus wants to show you how to love through a personal experience with Him, if you allow yourself to engage accordingly with Him on that level.

My question to you is have you had this experience? Have you experienced being in a love affair with Jesus? Do you long to commune with him, spend time with him?

Do you know what it's like to feel some type of way in your soul and Jesus the lover of your soul comes and comforts you and fills you from within?

If not, I beseech you to progress to a greater level of intimacy with your Savior and watch how much you become more rooted and grounded in love thus causing greater improvement in how you relate to others by way of love.

PONDER THIS: How do you demonstrate the love of God in the earth?

Thoughts of the Morning

Sharon R. Peters

Day 30

ARE YOU A FRIEND THAT CAN REPRESENT GOD TO YOUR FRIENDS?

About seven years ago I taught Excellence Classes to a group of women for one year. I titled one of the classes, BECOMING THE EXCELLENT FRIEND. I used the book of Job as my reference text and I highlighted how God instructed Job to pray for his friends and when he did the bible says God turned his captivity.

However, my thought today addresses Job's three friends. You all know the story of Job and how God suggested him to the devil for a series of afflictions. God had confidence that Job who was a righteous man and would hold fast to his integrity. Nevertheless, God did not like how Job's friends spoke about God as it relates to Job's time of trouble.

Listen to what God said to one of Job's friend after he got done dealing with Job:

Job 42:7 "After the Lord finished talking to Job, he spoke to Eliphaz from Teman. He said, "I am angry with you and your two friends, because you did not tell the truth about me, as my servant Job did."

My question to you today is this: Can you tell the

truth to your friends? Can you represent God in your friendships?

Or is this a grey area for you?

In every relationship that we as believers embark upon, God is looking for us to represent what is right in the sight of God. It doesn't matter what the relationship is, what matters is can we represent God who is truth in being.

Well Job's friends did not say what was right about God to him as he suffered. Job's friends did not represent God who is righteous and this angered God.

So look what God did,

Job 42:8 "So now, Eliphaz, get seven bulls and seven rams. Take them to my servant Job. Kill them and offer them as a burnt offering for yourselves. My servant Job will pray for you, and I will answer his prayer. Then I will not give you the punishment you deserve. You should be punished, because you were very foolish. You did not say what is right about me, as my servant Job did."

It was Job's prayer that saved his friends from being punished by God.

So when you are a godly friend, be sure to represent God righteously in your friendships, because God will hold you accountable if you misrepresent HIM even in friendship.

PONDER THIS: How can you be a better godly friend to your friends?

Day 31

WHEN AND WHERE IS YOUR PLACE OF MEDITATION?

Usually when I sleep God makes deposits or downloads into my spirit. Sometimes He enlightens me by way of dreams.

When I awake from sleep land, I've trained myself to go immediately into a place called meditation. It is in that place of meditation where I process the things that reside within my spirit.

Meditation is the place where I seek to gain understanding of that which God has placed within my spirit and that which he has shown me by way of dreams.

When I come out of meditation I enter into a time of devotion, searching out applicable scriptures that correspond to the revelatory downloads. I also study and look up words in the dictionary for more clarity. All of which I do right on my phone and I make the necessary notes accordingly, again right there on my iPhone.

Then I seek The Lord in prayer...

The culmination of all this results is this:

1. I usually come away from this time spent with God with a greater level of knowledge and understanding of his will.

2. I almost always learn something about me that I did not know or realize that lends to the "HD" of my life in Him.

3. Most times, my times of meditation causes me to grasp hold of a divine plan or strategy for successful implementation in my daily walk thus causing me to live THE GOOD LIFE IN HD regardless to the circumstances or situations of life.

PONDER THIS: How can you implement a purposed time of meditation in your day to "muse" on the things of God?

_____

_____

_____

_____

_____

_____

THOUGHTS OF THE MORNING

SHARON R. PETERS

MY FINAL THOUGHT

I truly believe that our thoughts govern our being. *Proverbs 23:7* lets us know that as a man thinks in his heart so is he.

My first thoughts in the morning are towards Him, God Almighty. I also believe that if I can get heavenly downloads and I meditate on these things, then I can govern my day with God's plans because His thoughts equate to His plans. God has a plan for your day and He wants you to think His plans daily!

In addition, I know without a doubt that God has a plan for my life but I must be willing to seek Him early in prayer but also in thought and meditation to know those plans since I endeavor to make every day count towards my purpose.

So sharing my morning thoughts has become a practice of mine. It's the way I commune with God when I awaken to a new day in Him.

Lastly, I thank you for journeying with me in thought and I pray that these inspired thoughts have encouraged, edified and even taught you something you didn't know already as you read a thought a day. I would love to hear your thoughts on this devotional so please contact me.

ABOUT THE AUTHOR

Apostle Sharon R. Peters is a set gift in the church. She was affirmed into the office of the Apostle in February of 2012 at 1:05 p.m. by Apostles C. Kevin and Candace Ford of Abiding Presence International Alliance (APIA). In December of 2012, Apostle Sharon (as she is affectionately called by the church) received her Doctorate of Divinity Degree from the Calvary School of Ministry for Independent Biblical Studies an affiliate of Grace Theological Seminary of Loris, South Carolina and most recently earned her Doctorate of Theology Degree from Open Arms International Bible College and Seminary School of Chicago, Illinois.

Apostle Sharon currently serves as a (Servant) Leader of The Empowerment Word & Truth Church (formerly Word & Truth Church) where she was installed as the Senior Pastor in 2008 by The Reverend Dr. Ramona Joseph of the African Pentecostal College of Bishops. She genuinely believes that NO ONE can die spiritually if they are connected to her for she loves to minister the bread of life and is a noted 21st Century Rebekah that can draw living water!

Prior to realization of her "divine purpose and calling" in the kingdom and the discovery of her ministry gifts, Apostle Sharon initially had aspirations of being a professional career businesswoman. In pursuit of her goals, she attended the University of Illinois Circle Campus and graduated with a Bachelor of Science Degree in Marketing. Upon entering the work force, Apostle Sharon was immediately recognized as a leader, a woman with an excellent work ethic and a strong mind for business. She quickly began her climb up the corporate ladder with one promotion after another, however, God had other plans for her and that was to build His Kingdom, not Corporate America. This was even more evident to Apostle Sharon after she received power through the baptism of the Holy Ghost and her life began to suddenly change as she moved in the direction of her divine calling and purpose.

She started her training and ministry work in Women's Ministry by assisting the Women's Ministry leader at her home church. Later, after it was prophesied that she had the "gift of administration and would be over many governments", and she began serving in an array of administrative capacities (from church announcer to Chairperson of the Board). Apostle Sharon has been very instrumental in using her gifts and abilities to organize and lead in women's ministry, effectively and efficiently manage church business, train and develop leaders to serve in ministry with a "Spirit of Excellence". She is also known for raising up ministry teams like Intercessory Prayer Teams and Apostolic Teams which are trained and set to accompany her on her many ministry assignments to help her do the work of ministry. Many have come to "hear" the gospel by way of her "voice" which God said he would use. Apostle Sharon is called upon often and sent by God to minister at Conferences, Church Services and Retreats and she is most known as an Apostolic Teacher and an Apostolic Mother to millions as was spoken by the Lord. In August of 2015, (as was prophesied) to her, Apostle Sharon walked through a "new door" as she ministered the word of God to over 9 million viewers on Trinity Broadcasting Network (TBN) in Ottawa, Illinois.

She has a caring and compassionate ministry for women and God uses her to birth out women onto the path of their purpose, dreams and destiny through her mentorship. Her purpose in photo-15life is to be the "standard of holiness" for women and because she understands the heart of a woman and she is anointed by God to bring about healing and restoration in the lives of women.

Apostle Sharon is the Founder/President of Sweet Rose of Sharon Women's Ministry, a place of feeding, a place to prepare for excellence & a place of healing and restoration. In addition, she has been noted for joining forces with the "Men of God" (especially those in senior leadership) in unity and agreement for the advancement of the Kingdom of God.

After five years of going it alone, in early 2013 the Lord caused her "Covenant Partner", Apostle Robbie C. Peters, of Kingdom Empowerment International Covenant Fellowship of Churches, Inc. to find her. Together they developed a close friendship as they joined in agreement to do the work of sent Apostles. In 2014, as love and purpose drew them closer they were united in Holy Matrimony and two became one flesh! Truly Apostle Sharon R. Peters is called to the kingdom for such a time as this!

Connect With Apostle Sharon:

Facebook: @livinglifeinhd
Twitter: @shruff2525
Web: www.livinginhd.org

Other Books Written by Apostle Sharon:

Teach Me How To Pray
Who Hurt The Church
The 3F's That Make For A Successful Christian

www.ingramcontent.com/pod-product-compliance
Lightning Source LLC
LaVergne TN
LVHW041256080426
835510LV00009B/753